W9-ANP-638

Road Trip: Famous Routes

The PAN-AMERICAN HIGHWAY

BY MARIA NELSON

Gareth Stevens
PUBLISHING

Library of Congress Cataloging-in-Publication Data

Names: Nelson, Maria, author.
Title: The Pan-American Highway / Maria Nelson.
Description: New York : Gareth Stevens Publishing, [2016] | Series: Road
 trip: famous routes | Includes index.
Identifiers: LCCN 2016011774 | ISBN 9781482446708 (pbk.) | ISBN 9781482446692 (library bound) | ISBN
9781482449471 (6 pack)
Subjects: LCSH: Pan American Highway System–Juvenile literature. | North
 America–Description and travel–Juvenile literature. | South
 America–Description and travel–Juvenile literature.
Classification: LCC E27.5 .N45 2016 | DDC 917.04–dc23
LC record available at http://lccn.loc.gov/2016011774

First Edition

Published in 2017 by
Gareth Stevens Publishing
111 East 14th Street, Suite 349
New York, NY 10003

Copyright © 2017 Gareth Stevens Publishing

Designer: Andrea Davison-Bartolotta
Editor: Kristen Nelson

Photo credits: Cover, p. 1 (bottom) Vadim Petrakov/Shutterstock.com; cover, p. 1 (top) Josef Hanus/Shutterstock.com;
p. 4 Joseph Sohm/Shutterstock.com; p. 5 Rosemary Calvert/Mobile Moment/Getty Images; p. 6 Chris Howey/
Shutterstock.com; p. 7 (map) Seaweege/Wikimedia Commons; p. 7 (background) Yobab/Shutterstock.com; p. 8 chris
kolaczan/Shutterstock.com; p. 9 Tony Ray/Shutterstock.com; p. 10 Nataliya Hora/Shutterstock.com; p. 11 EdgeOfReason/
Shutterstock.com; p. 12 littleny/Shutterstock.com; p. 13 Dorti/Shutterstock.com; p. 15 (main) Jess Kraft/Shutterstock.com;
p. 15 (inset) Yuri Cortez/AFP/Getty Images; p. 17 (main) Jonathan Mitchell/Moment/Getty Images; p. 17 (map)
ekler/Shutterstock.com; p. 18 Sergio TB/Shutterstock.com; p. 19 mezzotint/Shutterstock.com; p. 20 Family on Bikes/
www.familyonbikes.org; p. 21 Spiegl/ullstein bild/Getty Images.

Printed in the United States of America

CPSIA compliance information: Batch #CS16GS: For further information contact Gareth Stevens, New York, New York at 1-800-542-2595.

Contents

Words in the glossary appear in **bold** type the first time they are used in the text.

North to South

Can you imagine traveling from the tip of North America to the tip of South America? It's possible! There's a **route** that **stretches** from Alaska through Canada and the United States south into Mexico. It can then take you through Central America and down the west coast of South America, ending in Chile. It's called the Pan-American Highway!

This road trip would be a long, hard journey, but you would see so many different places and people along the way!

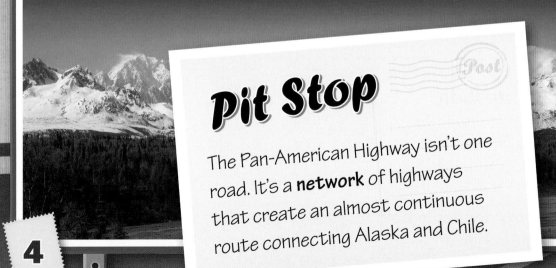

Pit Stop

The Pan-American Highway isn't one road. It's a **network** of highways that create an almost continuous route connecting Alaska and Chile.

All About the
Pan-American Highway

where found: from Alaska and northern Canada to the southern tip of Chile in South America

year built: first planned in 1923

length: nearly 30,000 miles (48,280 km), with a gap about 50 miles (80 km) long between Panama and Colombia

cities along the highway: Edmonton, Alberta, Canada; Salt Lake City, Utah; Las Vegas, Nevada; Guadalajara, Mexico; San Salvador, El Salvador; Lima, Peru; Santiago, Chile; Buenos Aires, Argentina

Along the Pan-American Highway are many major cities in North, Central, and South America.

The Route

The idea to build a highway stretching from North to South America first came about at a meeting of many countries in Chile in 1923. It took many years to **coordinate** the route.

Mexico built its part entirely, but the United States had to help some small Central American countries continue building the route. Even as recent as 1994, a piece was added so the route would start further north in the town of Deadhorse, Alaska! The end of the Pan-American Highway is in Puerto Montt, Chile.

Panama City, Panama

Pit Stop

One part of the Pan-American Highway is called the Inter-American Highway. It stretches from Nuevo Laredo, Mexico, to Panama City, Panama.

Some maps of the Pan-American Highway have differences, since it's not officially one road in some places. This map shows another part of the route between Edmonton, Alberta, and Dallas, Texas.

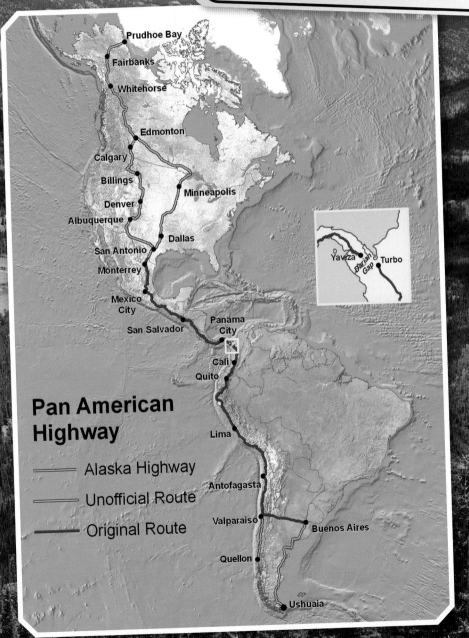

Prudhoe Bay
Fairbanks
Whitehorse
Edmonton
Calgary
Billings
Minneapolis
Denver
Albuquerque
Dallas
San Antonio
Monterrey
Mexico City
San Salvador
Panama City
Cali
Quito
Lima
Antofagasta
Valparaiso
Buenos Aires
Quellon
Ushuaia

Yaviza
Darían Gap
Turbo

Pan American Highway

═══ Alaska Highway

─── Unofficial Route

━━━ Original Route

A Cold Start

Alaska and northern Canada are beautiful places to visit! When traveling through them on the Pan-American Highway, road trippers need to keep the time of year in mind. Fairbanks, Alaska, near the start of the route, has an average low temperature of –17°F (–27°C) in January. But its average high in July is a comfortable 73°F (23°C)!

If you do travel through Canada during the winter, don't miss Edmonton. Snowshoeing and skiing are popular ways to enjoy the snow there.

Pit Stop

Near Edmonton, Elk Island National Park is a great place to spot wildlife such as bison, which went from being nearly **extinct** to increasing in population partly because of the park.

As far north as Fairbanks and Edmonton, you'll be able to spot the northern lights! You might have to stay up late, but seeing the colorful **aurora** is something you won't forget.

Stretch Your Legs

The Pan-American Highway route passes through several US states, including Montana, New Mexico, Colorado, and Nevada. Need to stop for some fresh air on your road trip? Denver, Colorado, is known for many hiking, biking, and climbing opportunities near the city.

Denver is close to the Rocky Mountains, including Rocky Mountain National Park. Visitors can fish in the more than 50 lakes and many streams in the park, and then camp at a campsite or in the backcountry among the trees.

Pit Stop

You won't see a sign for the Pan-American Highway in the United States. It simply follows certain roads in the US highway system.

Denver is called the Mile High City because it's found 1 mile (1.6 km) above sea level!

11

Bigger in Texas

Three of the top 10 most populated cities in the United States are in Texas—and two are found on Pan-American Highway routes. San Antonio, Texas, has more than 1.4 million people and a wonderful cultural history. You can learn a lot about Texas history there, from the San Antonio **missions** to the Alamo Shrine, the location of a famous Texas battle.

There's a lot to do in Dallas, Texas, too! Road trippers can take in a Cowboys football game or see the George W. Bush Presidential Library and Museum.

Pit Stop

Las Vegas, Nevada, is also on the route of the Pan-American Highway. Las Vegas is known for **entertainment**, so stop to see a magic show or eat at one of its many famous restaurants!

President John F. Kennedy was killed in Dallas. Today, visitors can learn more about the event and honor President Kennedy at John F. Kennedy Memorial Plaza.

Mexico City

On a road trip along the Pan-American Highway, you can't miss Mexico City, Mexico! There are many museums to learn about Mexican history and artists, as well as beautiful **architecture**. A big city square called the Zócalo has both ancient ruins and the offices of the Mexican government.

The Chapultepec Park and Zoo has one of the most visited zoos in the world. There are more than 2,000 animals, including Mexican wolves and giant pandas. The park around the zoo has a castle you can visit, too!

Pit Stop

When you cross into another country, you need to show a special **document** called a passport. It has your name, address, and picture on it. Be sure to get yours before heading out on the Pan-American Highway!

Mexico City is one of the largest cities in the world. More than 20 million people live there!

Through Central America

The route of the Pan-American Highway stretches down the Pacific coast of Guatemala, El Salvador, Honduras, Nicaragua, Costa Rica, and Panama. Bordered by the Pacific Ocean and the Caribbean Sea, there are many beaches to visit!

San Salvador, El Salvador, is known for nice beaches. But it's also near Coatepeque Lake, which was created by a **volcanic eruption** thousands of years ago! It's very deep, at almost 395 feet (120 m). The road leading to the crater shows off the best views of the lake.

Pit Stop

The Darien Gap in southern Panama has stopped many from traveling the whole length of the Pan-American Highway. It's only about 50 miles (80 km), but there's no way through the forest and over the rivers and streams there.

In 1960, someone did cross the Darien Gap in a car. But it took them almost 5 months!

Nicaragua

Carribean Sea

Costa Rica

Darien Gap

Panama

Venezuela

Pacific Ocean

Colombia

The South American Coast

Here are just a few of the cool places to visit on the Pan-American Highway route along South America's Pacific coast:

Isla de la Plata: See many different kinds of birds on this small island off the coast of Ecuador.

Lima, Peru: Learn about the **colonial** history of Peru at the Gold Museum and the great cathedral where Spanish explorer Francisco Pizarro is buried.

Viña del Mar, Chile: Visit one of Chile's beautiful coastal beaches or enjoy native flowers and plants at the national garden.

Lima is the capital city of Peru. It's a great place to stop and learn about the ancient Inca of Peru's past.

18

Pit Stop

For those who like to mountain climb, the Andes Mountains are a great place to use your skills! The Inca Trail in Peru takes you through the jungle and mountains and even to the ancient Inca city of Machu Picchu.

19

A Real Road Trip

Driving the entire Pan-American Highway would take months. That would take a lot of packing and planning. Now, imagine trying to travel the highway's length by bike!

One family from Idaho did just that! John and Nancy Vogel and their twin sons left from Alaska in 2008. At the time, the boys were only 10 years old! It ended up taking the Vogels 2 years, 9 months, and 13 days to complete the highway route by bike.

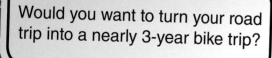

Would you want to turn your road trip into a nearly 3-year bike trip?

Road Tips
for the Pan-American Highway

Have Your Papers Ready: You'll need a passport, but you may also need other similar documents called visas for each country. The road trip driver might need a special **license**, too.

Stay Safe: Always lock your car. Keep money, cameras, and other costly items hidden, even when out walking.

Stop Car Trouble: Have a spare key as well as simple tools to fix common car problems.

Be Healthy: Get any shots you may need to keep from getting illnesses in certain countries. Know where it might not be safe to drink water and eat certain foods.

21

Glossary

architecture: the construction and style of a building

aurora: the occurrence of colors in the sky around Earth's poles

colonial: having to do with a colony, or a piece of land under the control of another country

coordinate: to bring into a common action

document: a formal piece of writing

entertainment: something that amuses or occupies others

extinct: no longer living

license: a document giving someone permission to do something

mission: places where Spanish settlers and priests lived and tried to spread Christianity

network: an interconnected group

route: a course that people travel

stretch: to reach across

volcanic eruption: the bursting forth of hot, liquid rock from within Earth

For More Information

Books

Petersen, Christine. *Learning About North America.* Minneapolis, MN: Lerner Publications, 2015.

Roumanis, Alexis. *South America.* New York, NY: AV2 by Weigl, 2014.

Websites

Central America
easyscienceforkids.com/all-about-central-america
Find out more about Central America for your travels!

South America Facts
kids-world-travel-guide.com/south-america-facts.html
Read about traveling in South America as well as facts about many of the countries the Pan-American Highway passes through.

Index